Mingle with the Mighty Troops of
GORILLAS

Published by Wildlife Education, Ltd.
12233 Thatcher Court, Poway, California 92064
contact us at: **1-800-477-5034**
e-mail us at: **animals@zoobooks.com**
visit us at: **www.zoobooks.com**

ISBN 1-932396-04-7

Gorillas

Created and Written by
John Bonnett Wexo

Scientific Consultants
Dennis A. Meritt, Jr., Ph.D.
Assistant Director
Lincoln Park Zoo

Diane K. Brockman
Curator of Mammals/Primates
San Diego Zoo and San Diego Wild Animal Park

Zoobooks

Contents

*G*orillas are high on the list of animals that people find most fascinating. For many people, gorillas are *the* most fascinating animals in the world. This is partly because gorillas seem to be so much like people.

When you see gorillas in a zoo, it is hard to escape the feeling that they are watching you as closely as you are watching them. They sometimes look back at you with so much interest and intelligence that you begin to wonder what they think of you. If gorillas could talk, they might turn to each other and say "what a strange human that is!"

The resemblance of gorillas and other great apes (chimpanzees and orangutans) to people is the reason they are called the *anthropoid* ("man-like") apes. Many tribes in Africa think of gorillas as primitive people, and the earliest explorers also thought that gorillas might be primitive, hairy people. In fact, the name *gorilla* was given to these animals by an explorer from ancient Carthage, who sailed along the west coast of Africa about 2,500 years ago. Literally translated, gorilla means "hairy person."

What are some of the things you notice about gorillas when you see them? Well, the first thing you probably see is that they are *big*. Gorillas are the largest of all primates—the family of animals that includes monkeys, apes, and humans. The average weight of an adult male gorilla is 340 pounds. Adult females are much smaller. They normally weigh about half as much as males. In zoos, males sometimes get very big indeed. The largest zoo gorilla on record weighed more than 750 pounds. But this was because the animal was overfed. In most zoos today, gorillas are not overfed, and they weigh about as much as wild gorillas.

The second thing you will probably notice about gorillas is that they are very *hairy*. All healthy gorillas have thick, springy hair covering most of their bodies. But adult gorillas do not have hair on the face, the chest, the palms of their hands, or the soles of their feet.

One of the most remarkable things about gorillas is something that you can't see by looking at them. They can live to be very old. In zoos, where they get good medical care, they may live more than 50 years.

A lowland gorilla

There are three types of gorillas in Africa. All gorillas are similar to each other in many ways, so most scientists say that all gorillas belong to a single group, or species. But there are some important differences between gorillas that come from different parts of Africa, so the scientists have divided gorillas into three regional types, or subspecies. These are called the Western Lowland gorilla, the Eastern Lowland gorilla, and the Mountain gorilla.

As you might guess from these names, some gorillas live at lower altitudes (lowland), while others live at higher altitudes (mountain). No matter what the altitude is, *all* gorillas live in very similar kinds of places—in dense forests, where there are many different kinds of plants. Gorillas are large animals, and they must have huge amounts of plant food to eat every day.

In the past, all three gorilla subspecies had much larger areas to live in than they have today. Their ranges may have been more than *twice* as large. As the weather in some parts of Africa grows drier, the forests grow smaller. People have started to cut down what remains of the great forests to make room for farms, to harvest timber, and simply for firewood. With every passing day, there is less room in Africa for the magnificent gorillas.

Eastern Lowland gorillas live in rain forests of central Africa. Their range is located more than 600 miles east of the Western Lowland gorilla's range. In general, eastern gorillas are a bit larger than their western cousins and darker in color. And there are fewer of them—probably only about 3,000 to 5,000 remain in the wild.

EASTERN LOWLAND GORILLA
Gorilla gorilla graueri

WESTERN LOWLAND GORILLA
Gorilla gorilla gorilla

Most gorillas in zoos are Western Lowland gorillas, which come from the tropical forests of West Africa. Although these are the smallest of the gorilla subspecies, a fully grown male may weigh more than 400 pounds. This subspecies has shorter hair than other gorillas, and the hair color may vary from black to grayish brown. The Western Lowland gorilla has the largest range (see map) and the largest population—about 35,000.

There are many similarities between both kinds of lowland gorillas. And there are many differences between lowland gorillas and mountain gorillas. It is easy to see some of these differences when you compare a male lowland gorilla (at left) with a male Mountain gorilla (below).

The head of a male Mountain gorilla is higher and more pointed, and his nose has a wider gap in the middle. Lowland males often have a patch of reddish hair on their heads, but Mountain gorillas do not.

■ WESTERN LOWLAND GORILLAS

■ EASTERN LOWLAND GORILLAS

■ MOUNTAIN GORILLAS

Mountain gorillas are the largest of all gorillas. Fully grown males may weigh more than 500 pounds. The hair on these gorillas is often very long and very black. They need long, thick hair because they live high in the mountains, where it can get cold. Their dark hair better absorbs heat from the sun and keeps their body heat from escaping. Mountain gorillas are the rarest of all gorillas. There are none in zoos and only abut 400 to 600 in the wild.

MOUNTAIN GORILLA
Gorilla gorilla beringei

9

Gorillas look like people in many ways. For example, they have two arms and two legs, with hands and feet that look similar to ours. A gorilla's head and body are also similar in many ways to a human head and body.

But there are many differences as well. For instance, a gorilla can use its feet to grab things. And the brain in a gorilla's large head is not as big as the human brain. On these pages, you'll find other similarities and differences.

Gorillas are much stronger than people. A fully grown male gorilla could easily win a tug of war with six men.

Unlike people, gorillas have bigger muscles in their arms than they have in their legs. In fact, the arm muscles of an average gorilla are stronger than the leg muscles of the strongest man. A large part of a gorilla's strength comes from its arms.

Under a gorilla's dark hair, the skin is also dark. Sometimes, baby gorillas are born with patches of pinkish skin that darken as they grown older.

Like people, gorillas can stand up on their legs. But they don't do it very often. When they walk, they almost always use their legs and their hands. In this "four-footed" position, it is easier for a gorilla to balance the heavy weight of its huge head and upper body.

Unlike people, gorillas have arms that are much longer than their legs. An average male gorilla is six inches shorter than an average man. But the gorilla's arms are about *one foot longer!*

The faces of gorillas are different from each other in the same way that human faces are all different. The best way to tell one gorilla from another is to look at their faces. Which one of these gorillas looks most intelligent? Which one seems angry? And which one appears to be thinking about something?

Most of a gorilla's bones and muscles are similar to yours, but the shape of the gorilla's body is different. For one thing, the stomach is much larger than the chest. This is because gorillas eat bulky food, and they need lots of room to hold all of it.

The hands of gorillas are similar to human hands in a number of ways. They have five fingers on each hand, with thumbs that can be used for grabbing things. They have fingernails instead of claws. And they have fingerprints that look like human prints. Can you see some ways in which gorilla hands are *different* from human hands?

When a gorilla walks, it uses the backs of its fingers like a foot. This is called *knuckle walking*. Gorillas and chimpanzees are the only animals that walk this way.

The **family** is the main social unit of gorillas. All gorillas live in family groups called *troops*, and these range in size from 5 to 30 gorillas. The head of each family is an adult male gorilla called a silverback. As a male grows older and stronger, the hair on his back slowly turns gray. By the time he has grown old enough to take command of a family, a male's back may be almost totally gray—and this is where we get the name "silverback."

Life in a gorilla family is usually very peaceful. Every gorilla seems to know its place in the order of things, and very little fighting takes place. The troop spends its days slowly wandering from place to place, eating as it goes. In many ways, gorillas seem to have the kind of simple life that some people say they would like to have.

The silverback is the strongest male in a gorilla group. It is his responsibility to protect the other members of the group if the need arises. For this reason, silverbacks are more aggressive than other gorillas, and more "touchy." A silverback can get very angry very fast.

At the end of every day, gorillas build nests for sleeping. They may build them on the ground or up in trees, and they use whatever materials happen to be handy.

Every gorilla has its place in the troop. The "boss" is the oldest male silverback. He may have several assistants that are called blackbacks.

SILVERBACK

BLACKBACK

FEMALE WITH YOUNG

FEMALE WITHOUT YOUNG

Females with babies have higher status than females that don't have them. There are usually twice as many females in a troop as males.

When a gorilla troop moves from place to place, the silverback usually takes the lead, followed by the other males, and then by the females. Wherever the leading silverback wants to go, the other members of the troop will follow.

Like people, gorillas use sounds and facial expressions to let others know what they are thinking and feeling. Here are some of the expressions that gorillas use. Can you tell what they are expressing?

1-ANGER, 2-HAPPINESS, 3-AGGRESSION, 4-ANXIETY

In general, gorillas in a troop treat each other with kindness and consideration. Even the powerful silverback may show gentleness and patience with the young.

The main activity of a gorilla's day is eating. Gorillas get up rather early and spend most of the morning eating. During the hottest part of the day, they take time off for a nap. After the nap, they keep eating until the sun goes down. During the course of a day, adult male gorillas can eat more than *40 pounds* of assorted leaves, stems, and roots from their favorite plants.

Gorillas really *love* to eat. As they chew, they often smack their lips together and grumble with contentment. Almost everything a gorilla eats comes from plants. Very rarely, they may eat a bird's egg or an insect. But 99 percent of their food comes from plants. To a gorilla, the dense forest is like a huge, green restaurant.

As a rule gorillas don't have to go very far to find food. They usually stay inside a rather small area called a *home range* ① and find everything they need. At certain times of the year, however, special foods may ripen outside the home range. The gorillas may travel some distance to get them ②. For example, Mountain gorillas may travel miles to get tender young bamboo shoots.

It is rare for gorillas to drink water in the wild. Most of the time, they get all the moisture they need from the plants they eat. Some of the juicier plants are almost half water.

Gorillas are fussy eaters. They know what they like, and that's all they will usually eat. With some plants, they may eat only the leaves. With others, only the stalk or the roots. As they eat, they may carefully stack the parts they don't want in a neat pile.

WILD BANANA

WILD CELERY

GINGER

TAPIOCA

Different types of plants are available in different parts of Africa, so gorillas that live in one place will have a different diet from gorillas that live elsewhere. But they all eat a wide variety of plants. Mountain gorillas eat *more than 100* types of plants, including the ones shown here.

Sometimes, a gorilla's strength comes in handy when searching for food. An adult male gorilla can easily tear a banana tree to shreds to get at the tender pith inside. Most of the time, gorillas need only a small part of their strength to get food.

Most of the plant food that gorillas eat is coarse and tough. But their strong jaws have no trouble grinding it up.

GORILLA

HUMAN

It's easy to see why the jaws of a gorilla are so much more powerful than human jaws. Gorilla jaws are much larger, with bigger teeth. Gorillas have huge muscles **①** to close their jaws. To see how muscles close jaws, feel the muscles on the side of your head **②** as you chew.

Baby gorillas are tiny when they are born. On the average, they weigh only 4½ pounds. If you consider that they may grow up to become 400-pound adults, you realize they have a lot of growing to do! They grow very fast.

Before long, the babies become active. Adult gorillas tend to be slow-moving and reserved in their behavior. But young gorillas are just the opposite. They scamper around among the adults in search of as much fun as they can find. In general, the life of a young gorilla is a happy one, filled with all kinds of discoveries.

Like almost all baby animals, newborn gorillas are very easy to love. They have big, dark eyes and sweet expressions that make them impossible to resist.

To help it cling to its mother, a newborn gorilla has a powerful grip. It can use both its hands and its feet to grab its mother's hair.

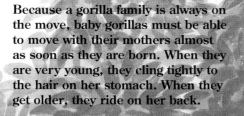

Because a gorilla family is always on the move, baby gorillas must be able to move with their mothers almost as soon as they are born. When they are very young, they cling tightly to the hair on her stomach. When they get older, they ride on her back.

Gorilla babies and human babies develop in similar ways during their first year. But the baby gorillas develop much *faster*. As you can see, they can do many things long before human babies can do them. By the end of the year, the mental development of gorillas slows down, and the human babies pass them by.

CRAWLING
9 WEEKS

STANDING
20 WEEKS

WALKING
34 WEEKS

CRAWLING
37 WEEKS

STANDING
43 WEEKS

WALKING
52 WEEKS

Like human children, young gorillas like to wrestle and tumble around a lot.

Older gorillas are too large and heavy to do much tree climbing, but young gorillas do a lot of it.

An unusual game of young gorillas is the "conga line." They form a chain and walk through the forest.

In the wild, gorilla mothers learn how to care for their babies by watching other mothers. In zoos, there may not be other mothers to watch, so zoo keepers sometimes try to show new mothers what they should do.

Like human babies, young gorillas like to "wear" their food. This baby has made a fine hat out of a banana leaf.

Gorillas and people should be friends. After all, gorillas have many traits that we should admire. For one thing, they are generally peaceful animals. When they are left alone, they rarely bother anyone. Although they have tremendous strength, they rarely use it to hurt other creatures. There is a lot of evidence that gorillas are very intelligent. They seem to live in an intelligent way.

Certainly, these are animals that we should learn to know better—and help to protect.

If you want to befriend a gorilla, act like a gorilla. Field scientists have found that the animals will let them get close if the scientists do things that gorillas do. If you meet a gorilla, here is what you should do.

In the past, people took pride in killing gorillas. Hunters thought of gorillas as dangerous "big game" and tried to shoot as many as they could. Now that we know more about gorillas, the time has come to treat them in an entirely different way.

If a silverback successfully scares away intruders, he doesn't try to hunt them. He calmly turns and wanders into the forest.

Most people have seen pictures of big gorillas beating their chests and charging— a frightening sight. But gorillas are not really violent animals. When they charge, they are simply trying to scare away intruders.

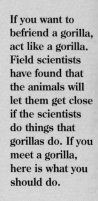

20

Never stare at a gorilla. A gorilla never looks directly at another gorilla unless it wants to fight. Look out of the corner of your eye.

[s]tay down. Be quiet. A gorilla that stands up [a]nd gets noisy is usually angry. If you stand up [a]nd are noisy, a gorilla will think you are angry.

Eat a leaf. To gorillas, this is a very peaceful gesture. Gorillas that eat together are usually friendly.

Scientists who have been studying Mountain gorillas have shown the gorillas that people are not always violent and destructive. As a result, certain groups of gorillas will let people get close to them. They are curious about us, too.

In zoos, gorillas and people have been looking at each other for many years. When you look at these pictures of gorillas that were taken in zoos (above and below), it's clear that the gorillas find us just as interesting—and perhaps as amusing—as we sometimes find them.

21

The future of gorillas depends on the survival of the forests in which they live. All three subspecies can only find the food they need in dense forest, so they will surely die out if all the forests are cut down.

Unfortunately, this is just what is happening in many parts of Africa. Trees are cut down—at an alarming rate—to make room for farms and to sell the timber. There is a need for more farmland, because the human population of Africa is growing rapidly. Every year there are more people, and more food must be produced to feed them. In parts of Mountain gorilla range, hundreds of thousands of war refugees have laid bare thousands of acres of forest. They cut the trees for firewood to cook their food.

The growing human population often turns cattle into the remaining forest, and the cattle eat the plants that gorillas normally eat. This deprives the gorillas of food. In some parts of Africa, gorillas are killed as food for humans.

The most endangered of the gorillas are the Mountain gorillas. The entire population of these magnificent animals is found in only a few small forests of the neighboring countries of Rwanda, Zaire, and Uganda. Population studies in the early 1960s estimated that there were at least 5,000 Mountain gorillas and maybe as many as 15,000. Today, the entire Mountain gorilla population numbers 400 to 600 animals living in a 285-square-mile area. The governments, game rangers, and conservation workers that oversee that area are dedicated to the preservation of Mountain gorillas. But in 1995, seven gorillas were killed by poachers—three in Zaire and four in Uganda. It was the first time in 10 years that Mountain gorillas had been poached in either country.

Western Lowland and Eastern Lowland gorillas are better off. There are more of them, and their ranges are much larger. But forest destruction, if it's allowed to continue, will eventually place them in the same position as Mountain gorillas.

To save gorillas in the wild requires that they have adequate forest habitat. Without that, the only hope is to save the species through captive breeding. Many zoos now breed and raise Western Lowland gorillas. They have not had the opportunity to try captive breeding with Eastern Lowland or Mountain gorillas.

Gorillas are peaceful creatures. If people are willing to leave them a place to live, without bothering them, they will continue to survive, as they have for millions of years.

Index